Confessio Armantis

BY

Socrteez

ENCHANTED MUZE PUBLISHING ♦ HOUSTON

Copyright © 2015, Sean A. Thomas
All rights reserved. No part of this publication may be reproduced, stored in a retrieval system or transmitted in any form or by any means, electronic, mechanical, photocopy, recording or otherwise, without prior written permission from the publisher, with the exception of short excerpts used with acknowledgement of publisher and author.

Printed in the United States of America

Confessio Armantis
ISBN: 978-1-930112-40-7

Enchanted Muze Publishing
E-mail: thadoubleh@gmail.com

Cover Design and Photography:
Heathens House A&E Group

10 9 8 7 6 5 4 3 2 1

This book is dedicated to
my boys
the girls
my rose
and
the love of a lifetime
I pray we continue to make beautiful art

Contents

Artistic Appeal	1
Emergency Transmission	9
The Public Address	14
Eye Am	21
Already Learned	28
Airborne	31
Access: Denied	34
Eye Wish	40
Mermaid	43
Cents of Freedom	47
Elephants & Ants	52
Excuse Me Miss	59
Free Falling	64
Hatin' Remedy	68
I Hope So	71
In Passing	75
Laujikwurx	80
Satin Stains	84
Sounds of Blackness	88
Sticks & Stones	92
Still	97
Metamorphosis	99

The Lost City	101
Colors	104
Altered Reality	108
Pink Slip	113
Cybernetic Cypher	121
Love Dance	125
Sentimental	128
The Successful Failure	130

Artistic Appeal
...in Poetry

I remember the moment I wanted to become a writer. I was fifteen years old, and I had just been blown away by "The Ballad of Dorothy Parker", by Prince. Although I had been a connoisseur of music at an early age (thanks primarily to my father), I had never been so drawn to a song! I was blown away by...and that's when things got "complicated". For the first time in my life, my vision of the song extended beyond the mere melody. More than just the words...more than just the music...more than the two working together so perfectly as to paint the picture in your mind with every measure...more than a melody that plays in your mind long after it's finished, but begins as if there is no end. More than all of this, I began to create an entirely new story!

In the past, I began life 'in song' as an "extra". As the song played, I could see the image, but I was never a part of the story. "Crazy Train" by Ozzie Ozbourne, is a perfect example of my simply standing in the scene. The train was moving, yes, but I wasn't on the train nor was I 'in control' of it. I was an observer of the "main characters", but I was not the star. However, as I began to grown in music, I graduated to a "stand-in" role. I studied the script and I was "invited" to the story, thus becoming a part of it. As I began to study the purpose of melody to sound equations, pitch to tone theories, and a host of other elements that defines "aesthetically pleasing" in music, I began to elevate my "expectation" of the art. Soon, I accepted the leading role and the main character was me! I became the lonely "Man on the Corner" by Genesis...I was the frustrated guy bangin' on the drums (although I couldn't play, nor had a clue Phil Collins was singing a song about divorce) "In the Air" tonight...I was the guy with Lucy & Cynthia Rose having "Starfish & Coffee". As much as I was the lead character, I was still nothing more than an actor in a script written by someone else.

When the last note to the ballad had been played, seemingly the song didn't stop. It continued on somewhere in my mind that not only had its own set design, but the characters were already in place! The song extended onward so, that not only was I offered the opportunity to pen the rest of this beautifully un-ending silent film that has a supplied soundtrack, but I was up all flippin' night from the excitement. A rush had come over me so severe, I literally woke up the next morning like a kid on Christmas morning. A writer was born that night, but it has taken several years for me to even feel comfortable telling people I'm a "writer". My skills were refined from criticism both in and out of art. My television viewing changed. What used to be greeted with utter disdain suddenly became a welcomed subject (for whatever reason). I took notice to what "appealed" to the senses. I noticed that my objections to previously presented sounds, were then investigated & re-catalogued. What could have been 'offensive' to the pallets, were tasted again to ensure "quality assurance". I examined everything I ingested and graded all that crossed my path. Being the agent of chaos that I am, I questioned others as to why they "accepted" what was being fed to them, regardless the source.

Seemingly, my generation has ushered in an age of media dependency, and the public appeared to me as "zombies" dancing to whatever tune the piper's were playing. The more I examined the content of the messages being sent through main stream media, my depression grew greater from the impending doom that was soon to appear. When "quality entertainment" is defined by planted ex-convicts who portray role models for separation purposes, drug abusive under-acting individuals whose lives will never be perfect, and power hungry horemongers who inaccurately define success, it's a wonder why society has issues defining beauty…it's a wonder as to why it's complicated to define beauty in one's message (art). Art, like life, is not complicated…it is the combination of simplicities working in concert to produce a compelling appeal to the witness of said work. Even the most putrid of products can contain an appealing element that both attracts & entraps a witness. The question that must be answered by onlookers is what is the "separator"? Where is the line drawn, when it comes to whether a work "works" or not?

Plato emphasized proportion, harmony and unity when examining aesthetics. Aristotle exhumed the notions of order, symmetry and definiteness. By definition, aesthetics is pertaining to, involving, or concerned with pure emotion and

sensation as opposed to pure intellectuality. So then, art is nothing more than a message from one sender to a receiver that "should" appeal to the senses. Is anyone paying attention to the plural tense in 'senses'? If there are five (5) senses...if we perceive by way of our senses...our perceptions mold & churn our beliefs...then, would it not make sense to be attentive to **ALL** the "senses" are processing with any communication, be it art or otherwise? The purpose of any work of art, is to transmit a message. The appeal of that message is largely induced by the level of the witness. What is the message's meaning? Is the meaning congruent with what the senses perceive? Is that message being conveyed correctly?
There are a number of 'needs' that require attention in terms of the message, but the sole heir of the "is the message being properly presented", rests on the presenter...the artist. What motivates the artist, and is that motivation visibly apparent in the work...or does it linger in

the shadows? Is the message's intent clear? The more elements added to the piece, the more "dimensionality" is added. As in other aspects of life, art is not exempt from the asinine ideology that more is better. Too often, artist (including myself) are guilty of over-indulging in the gluttony of an audience's accolades, we completely disrespect the craft (whatever craft we partake in). We drag story lines out that should have been cut...we sing too many runs in a too long song...we add too much color to a perfect picture. By adding more than should exist, we destroy the beauty of perfection and reduce & demean the work to a 'novelty' item as opposed to a collectible.

If we are to produce a better society, then we should be creating better artists. Along with creating better artists, we should also be demanding of the art we **DO** ingest! If poetry is an 'elevated' form of artistic expression, then there is a charge...a call...a responsibility to produce work that either questions, answers or possess a quality that contains elements of both as well as entertain. We who would call ourselves "poets" or those who seek to join the ranks of those regarded as poets, are educational entertainers who appeal to those who would hear. We are creative expressionist who paint pictures with our pens and make magic with our words. We are more than mere puppets for claps & finger snaps...we are not rappers. We are defenders of the truth. So, why are SO many of us feeding the foolishness?

S.A. Thomas

Emergency Transmission

i find comfort in knowledge
...
sifting sands which seek shelter amidst
hollow walls with shallow centers that
favor weak foundations

ever notice how nature yields to that which
is natural?
the presence of you in, is only
needed for survival
what is to be nurtured?
notating this a spiritual battle,
not a religious war,
is not witnessing such duplicity disturbing?
prostration featuring elation braced by
adoration,
should only be offered to The Worthy
what manner of man can accept such
praise?

titles are given to anyone wanting
hence they are called the willing
which puzzled peace do you choose?

a sycophantic grain of salty sand is
all that i am in a strangely
savage and insecure land
when wealth is the stronghold of the soul,
even sanctuaries are littered by an
overflow of sin
erecting from the bowels of ignorance,
society has systemically
substituted fact with hypocritically crafted
veracity
offering white noised fiction for intelligent
sound
how does one intimately understand what
real is?

proud parents promote their productions
however, when you are nobody's child,
who's bastard are you?
silent support sounds much like life is
phased by mute

while seeking assistance in the search of you,
an astute understanding of self is the most proper tool
when your system's design base is supposedly faith,
define God in you if blaspheme is the only unforgivable sin
whispered words that descend like snow are varied at best
beset wayfaring destinations not known
heat needed for physical existence send smoked
signals that mimic inhaled aspirations
sweetly marinated confusion crafted by the makers of
comical conclusions that
slowly bond with my bone
examine my nest only to notice,
that yet again i am on my own
how am i to find comfort in an honorable death,
when that journey is to be suffered alone?
as opposed to free falling from forest green code,

understanding may be better flowing once
you employ
elevated characters
remove the idological assets that keep you
concentrated in the Matrix, and perhaps
there may be
some validity in a little blue pill

still, it's hard to access who you are,
when others offer offensive kisses that
leave you
continuously curious
when very few know my ambitions
and even fewer know of my plans,
to say that you are intimate with my moves
is to offer you know more of me than i
ever can
i cannot stand the actions of an idiot
nor those that follow a fool
bejeweled by boothes bounty,
my hands are coated in the
essence of equality's economics
thirty dirty pieces of plasma stained
beads are ransomed for me
to embalm a bandit's pleasure

i am nothing more than a muted memoire
reminiscent of judas' treasure
sold into overzealous persecution,
my prosecution has been laboriously swift
like an autumn breeze blown by a tropical force,
my winds can hardly be considered stable
a summer's ease is explored on the
eve of a hueless blood moon
soon,
every fort night finds me hunting fictitious creatures
on the dark side of forces concealed
seeking solace in someone who simply
wants me plainly
simple is something i have never been
synonymous with
so close to stupidity
so close to insanity

The Public Address

There are a number of prophecies
implanted in my belief system
and trust that I live in accordance to each
One, a man aint to piss in the wind
Two, if u find urself in a ditch, stop diggin'
and
Three, if u think urself 2 notably ahead, u probably r
operating under the assumption that u've moved 2 far
Pace ur thoughts ur words and ur actions
Life is 2 short, this is a recession ... nigga,
aint no time for relaxin'
Time, is a luxury a black man cannot afford
An idle mind Is the devil's workshop, so I
should never fashion my lips 2 utter I'm bored
oh yeah ...

I got 1 more ...
Never waist a thousand dolla word on a 2 dolla whore
So, don't start no shit, there won't be no shit
and if ur taking time 2 color in the lines 2 out-do mines,
trick u truly need 2 quit
I'll take ur material
reanimate it so ruff that it finally makes sense,
causing u 2 choke on ur own spit

It's SocraTeez ... Dr. Pleasure ... Captain Nemo ... Mr. 151
Many, know of me as a heathen, simply because I love 2 have fun
It's the Supreme Rhetorical Master at ur service, and although u shouldn't piss on urself in fear, bitch u should be nervous
be afraid ... be very afraid

You see
2 many fraudulent falsifiers have stood behind the mic and exaggerated on their

clits & cocks in a lame attempt to garner more applause from the audience during a show, so their ego's can feel hot
Seriously?
Then have the nerve 2 ask what's the difference between them & me?
the fact that Teez aint ever lied
Even when it cums 2 my "climatic" skills, 98% of the women who have walked away, have left moaning satisfied
And seeing as how I don't like 2 leave a job undone ...
yes dear, I love 2 see my missions thru ... please believe u me, I'm still working on the other 2

See, me
I'm the kinda guy that doesn't deal in games ... I simply let the bullshit be
The kinda cat that, if she said her name was Trinity, ask her if my name was Neo ... could we meet in the middle of the Matrix around 3
There's a reason why a few refer to me as the "Head Heathen" baby ...

I'm a cliterologist
Personal trainer 4 ur pussy's fitness
and since I plan on exploring the depths of the
beautiful body of water between ur knees,
call me Captain Nemo, ur intimate exhibitionist
I likes 2 be real with mines ... speaking of which,
it's time 2 drop the subtleties and complementing comments ...
I'm ready 2 dive into u like a free-form diver in the Olympics
be so deep in u till ur xyphoid process sings
send distress calls 2 u by way of ur spine
while we're doing the damn thing
absorb every juicy drop u got, till u gotta pull me out with a string

Don't ask me what I want, cuz questions aint what I'm trying 2 get
Just, place my stick wherever u think I'll get the best form fit
hell, my hand's are tired honey

may I borrow ur mouth 4 a minute?

suck
take it 2 the head like a big gulp till u
getta brain freeze from my pleasure type
suck
till u make like Old Faithful and shoot a
geyser full of cum thru a straw type
fuck
girl look ... making love is a metaphor 4
what we did last night ...
2nite, we 'bout 2 get buck type

"ALL HANDS ON DECK"
will serve sound as the call 4 the crew 2
man their positions
girl, u grab the stern
I'll offer the orders
and we'll dive into the wet waves of
ecstasy with erotic precision
I'm just saying though ... u may be
pleased ... who knows
Subsequently, please be advised of page 9
section A:
I am not responsible 4

temporary hearing loss, massive muscle
spasms, cardiac arrests
OR
the permanent curling of toes

I go by many names and I've been called
many things that
at 1 point was probably true
However, I'm nothing more than a man
who passed by a mirror,
looked down and noticed the dirt on my
feet and
shit ... the mess on my shoulder's 2
Be it at the round table, diner 4 2 or dine
alone,
it's ur call as 2 what makes it 2 ur plate

Hi, I'm Soc 4 the homies
Teez 2 the ladies
Captain Nemo, the Ambassador of
Adventure, to date
Dr. Please, Psy D., the cliterologist,
the sensuous professional who keeps u
comin' pretty straight
Mr. 151, 2 much 4 ur tongue

or simply
SocraTeez
the muthafuckin'
Head of State

#

On any given Sunday, the sun can be seen
setting in the west
after rising in the east
(a small price to pay for commanding peace)
Brief glimpses of greatness rise from
meaningless sex stained sheets
that cover flesh trained briefs
all in search of Solomon's lost key
Spend every dime
exhaust both energy & time
to force open a third eye
merely but for a five minute dream
And it seems
some still cannot see me
Lite speed is rather fast, so screw it
eye am your epiphany's fantasy
kiss me on my ego

So serious
Circumcise your mind
eyem a miracle making melody maker
eye can redirect your kind, redefine reality
Take three lefts so eye can right
as eye remix time
A walking contradiction…black man with
blue blood who bleeds red
My reflection resembles Pinhead
However, this façade is adequate or so
eye've heard it said
Hannibal Lecture is a colleague,
so lessers become banana bread biscotti's
for my
Jamaican Blue Mountain coffee with
Parisian almond crème & toffee
eye am the double headed demon who
saves
Change the game with a wave of my hand
who craves
Thus, be it resolved, eye am reality at its
finest
Your land is my domain
eye am pharaoh reborn

eye am your highness
eye am the reason non-singing lames are singing in the first place
If you take a pile of pooh
spray paint it platinum, you will still have nothing more
than a pretty pile of shit...please
Cornbread, Earl, Hi-C & Me
We made sure the scene was supplied with banging beats
we wrote the blueprint on
"How To Make Your Poetry Show Hot: Even When the Shit on Your List Is Not"
eye am not that nigga, although eye am the O.N.E.
Hell, eyem the reason why they offer disclaimers at shows son
prick please
nothing more than a flea to me
eye electrify audiences like Blanka baby
act like you know
eyem an uncanny x-man well beyond super,
eyem an extraordinary hero

Call me Mr. Manhattan, because eye can
make incredulous things happen
Hey, eyem the reason pussy-hunting
pretenders defecting to rapping
they aint got nuts like these
Spend their child's support change to
download a lyricist greatest hits collection
on mp3, only to read the biography and
discover their favorite artist's favorite
artist is SocraTeez

Eye handle my bitch problem one flea at a
time
Wondering if eyem going to get mines, is
like tweeting the Brothers Johnson and
Jesus to see if the son is going to shine
get the funk out my face
Eyem so ahead of you hoes, eyem bungee
jumping on Jupiter broadcasting live in HD
from space
You can still keep up with a sundial, it's
true
a non-commissioned analogue is right
once in a while
every dog has its day

eye imagine its only fair that this principle applies to a bitch too
eye am this game and this game is me
eyem so art
eye inhale society's tells and piss filtered fantasies that echoes a drunk mans cream dreams
eye secrete seduction and feed from Despair in apologetics
eye am poetry, so when eye inhale putrid past lives that amount to humorous lies, eye filter the foolishness and exhale aesthetics
eye am having tea in the Sahara with Peter Parker & Ciara, and they are referring to me as Dr. Stephen Strange
strange...but eye know you see it
eye am life, liberty and the pursuit of freedom
you heard right,
eye am poetry

So, play your position trick and treat the game with a little more respect
You have been begging for the real...

Well, this shit right here...is about as real
as it gets
colder than the cum from iceman's dick,
trick, eye may be an ass...never an anus,
but bitch eye aint shit to play with
eye"ll make you famous...hello hoe
ask your girl if eyem not her biggest secret
Even when you go hard
she's still thinking about me
eye am the plumb line, the cleaner and the
waiter
if poetry is my Stars Wars, then Luke,
eye am your father
eye am Lord Vader

Both maniac and braniac
beautiful nightmare
king of beast
you are a pussy being fed by a griffin,
if we are what we eat
eye am the trillion dollar O.G.
and you...you are a four dollar jigga
look well beyond the frame
eye know you see it
eye am a North African Albino,

when eye go ape my nigga
eye am nirvana
so, eye am Billy Badass' superlative figure
King Kong, Mighty Joe Young and Godzilla
pay homage to me baby,
because eye go-realla

Already Learned

The left hand of Fate
swung at me,
making me move
to the right
Quiet is Despair
and her sister Delight
Limbo, a chamber of
nothingness, must
be my resting place
For it seems I have
fought Fate, and
Fate has won
(for now)
He seizes victory from my
grasp and punishes me
to my Hell
Was it something I said?
Could it be that I offended Him?
"No time for thought", says Destiny

"You must move thinking
only on your next action"
My last,
is in the past
and the past is behind me
Concentrate on the things before me
and my wondering ways will
be no more
(or so I've heard)
With the extension of His right,
Fate opens a door and
tells me to make
haste
Sit idle for no one,
lest I take rest
but rest is never given
to one who wrestles
with Fate
The only things that
await me are
headaches,
hard times
and harsh words
Will I be freed?
maybe, maybe not

Will I suffer?
maybe, maybe not
Will I stop fighting Fate?
maybe, maybe not
but one thing is certain
As the hour-glass moves,
I shall have no reprieve
or light
till I learn to stop
and fold the fight

Airborne

There were a
flock of seagulls
overhead
The sky was
gray
and no rays shined
Through the clouds
a dark and dismal day
it was, and someone said
look to the hills
In the hills,
a storm brewed and the
lightning made itself known
The wind rushed over
my head and birds were in
motion
It seemed so sensible
seemed so sensible

so sensible
sensible
With the storm coming, take flight
Mount up my wings and take flight
With the storm coming, take might
Make my move with all my might
With the storm coming, take light
In the midst of darkness, be bright
On this dark and dismal day,
moving seems so
irrational
So irrational, my mind is floating
But...
my flight, my flight
with all my might
I shall take my wings
and fly to Light
leave the gray skies
and in darkness be bright
Though it may take
all my might
There were a
flock of seagulls
overhead
The sky was

gray
and no rays shinned
through the clouds
sensible
so sensible
seemed so sensible
it seemed so sensible
and it begins

Access: Denied

I held her with my hands softly,
as my left crept past the curves her body conferred
and as these gifted fingers found their way to
sensuous spots her delicate design tried to conceal,
she could still feel the moisture from my tongue as my lips had yet again found hers
A small eruption of erotic proportion flew from her lips as her "moans" turned to "purrs",
causing her to call the only name that matters at this moment
and I ...
I could have sworn it was you
Instantly, this deserted island I had yet to explore,

became familiar land to me as
my ears began to recall what you felt like
my nose began to remember what you taste like
my hands began to render what you sound like
my tongue began to revive what you look like
Suddenly, I found myself lost at sea
diving to dared depths deeper than where low emotions rest

This, must be some screwed up test, because you ...
you shouldn't be here
You left that pier long ago
and although you know I love you,
one of us needs to exit stage left of this scene
and be damn if it's going to be me
she ... deserves better
my soul, should be stronger
however
yes dear ... this is what you wanted
and no matter how hard I've fronted,

your permission is accepted no longer

I was roaming out of range
and never could get a clear signal
regarding
the haterocity garnered by my new friend
and me ...
I mean we ... "we" were really green during
those days
but looking back at it, you were right ... it
was all me!
it was me who suffered
it was me who lost
it was me who was torn between my
heaven and my hell
and
it was me who paid the recessive cost
it was me who moved
it was me who tried
It was me,
who's Hope was disturbed by a thief in the
night,
strangled ... suffocated ... and died
Yeah, I lied ... but then again, you did too
peace is a beautiful thing though

In spite of it all, I sleep well at night
sweetheart ... how about you?
I imagine it must be real difficult adjusting
to the light
Just because you can see clearly in the
Matrix my love,
it doesn't mean that you have sight
One of us needs to steer clear of this
scene,
and be damn if it's going to be me
she ... deserves better
my soul should be stronger
but baby, this is what you wanted
and no matter how hard I've fronted,
your permission is accepted no longer

I have, however, carried on as if you never
mattered
as though your name was nothing more
than a mere memory ...
surrounded by laughter ...
like life without loving you can hardly be
considered living ...
like my last breath was not supposed to be
used while we were kissing ...

like I never knew how much I depended on
your smile to breath
(something's missing)
Yet, lest we forget, I am the one with the
problem, right?
Remember what's done in dark closets
dear ...
they do make their way to the light

Our love story was supposed to be the
sweetest love song the world has ever
known ... now, it's nothing more than a
cautious recollection in my mind
And from time to time, I'm inclined to
believe that
I wouldn't recognize who in the hell I've
become,
even after staring at my own reflection
but I
...
I am thru playing with Love's "false
impressions"
I am willing, wanting & waiving
I am willing to let you be free
I am wanting "we", to be removed from me

and
I am waiving ... good life my love
because she ... deserves better
my heart is stronger

This is what you wanted and for far too damn long,
I've lied to myself and fronted
I cannot crown a woman who refuses to be queen ...
not even in my dreams ... trust me, I've tried
your permission is accepted no longer
your access, has been denied

Eyewish

eye wanna be the air u breath

eye wanna be ur everything

for u there's nothin' eye won't due

been everything for u baby...including ur

fool

smelling sumthin' familiar

tasting u on my tongue

reachin' out for u lady

but eyem seein' no one

eye wish eye didn't love u so much

eye wish eye didn't long for ur love

eye wish eye didn't need u so much

eye wish eye didn't need ur touch…

ur taste…ur kiss…baby eye miss us

eyem staring pictures

inside empty frames

see u everywhere eye go

think eyem goin' insane

u're the star in my dreams

although eye don't know why

holdin' on to u baby

to everything u & eye

eye wish eye didn't love u so much

eye wish eye didn't long for ur love

eye wish eye didn't need u so much

eye wish eye didn't need ur touch…

ur taste…ur kiss…baby eye miss us

livin' without u

seems eyem takin' all the blame

eyem hearing one 2 many voices

girl eyem cryin' out ur name

wanna kiss u

girl eye miss u

what more can eye say?

eye wish eye didn't love u so much

eye wish eye didn't long for ur love

eye wish eye didn't need u so much

eye wish eye didn't need ur touch…

ur taste…ur kiss…baby eye miss us

mermaid

livin' in fracture inside hope's hip
eyem about to board this rockin' ship
payin' no neva mind 2 what eye left behind
oh eye feel the sun...seemingly eye can't see
how eyem 'sposed 2 sail this untamed sea
sea of stupidity that's been muddied by lies

eye believe in fairytales
but eye refuse 2 believe
that my dreams and desires
got the better of me
waitin' for the for the fog 2 lift so eye can
finally be free...be free

promise me baby
promise me
promise me

promise me baby
that ur love will stay real...awh stay real
promise me baby
promise me
promise me
promise me baby
forever's until

wicked waves eye ride 2 escape homeland harms
seems like eye've sailed inside the perfect storm
wonder how long can eye stay in her eye
my crew staged a coop, no one left but me
seems ignorance ushered in a mutiny
how'eyem 'sposed 2 make it all alone, God only knows

eye believe in fairytales
but eye refuse 2 believe
that my dreams and desires
have got the better of me

what 2 do what 2 due
what to...gotta trust u

promise me baby
promise me
promise me
promise me baby
that ur love will stay real...awh stay real
promise me baby
promise me
promise me
promise me baby
forever's until

seems like eye lost my sails
eyem being carried by the wind
eye rise from below deck
hit the next wave 'for it begins
what 2 do
what 2 due
oh Lord, how do eye not lose?

promise me baby
promise me
promise me
promise me baby
that ur love will stay real...awh stay real

promise me baby
promise me
promise me
promise me baby
forever's until

Cents of freedom

In the majority of my endeavors,
I have often attempted to demonstrate
(to the best of my abilities)
an unrelenting determination to be forthcoming
in my desire to be free
However, I have become a caged beast
entrapped by my passions
...
enslaved by my lusts
It would appear perfectly plausible then
that this pleasure would be my paradox ...
that which I would always imagine, but never possess
Like a carpenter's concept ...
an inventor's idea ...
a politicians promise ...
I too think valiant thoughts,

but those thoughts never
align with a ray of light
Maybe I have lived on the dark side too long

Whatever the case may be, I am what I appear
to be because Time has taught me
to be the me you see

Freedom is a slave song sung
by patrons from the past
Just as Liberty & Justice are twin
prostitutes walking the same beat,
but standing at opposite corners of the block ...
My broke ass ran out of gas somewhere
between those two hoes and Lord knows I can't
sing that damn good to raise my spirit
from the hood
and
Unity
...
she's the madam in this Moulin Rouge of

societal blues that keeps us erect waiting for the
next chorus line to begin
Hell, I've been waiting for her to bless my eyes
every since I was able to compromise my
fantasies for Duty and those damn two twins
Someone said they saw her swing her hips in at about
6:19 ... personally, that someone has to be mistaken because
things are just as chaotic as the day I began

What to do ... What to damn do?

Sometimes I rethink thoughts of whether or not
I developed on the right/wrong side of the tracks
In fact, periodically I want to drown in my despair
contemplating how much my checking account lacks

At this point, I'm believing that it's better this way …
if my available funds were visible, would I want to be
fucked by Liberty & Justice today?
This depleted deficiency I display keeps me in check,
like a tight fitting dog collar wrapped around my neck
At about 9:11, Unity finally stepped over to me and said,
"Dear, you appear to be bored. Would you care
for a drink or something to eat?"
I told her no thank you, but I would gladly take some sovereignty
The waitress brought over a huge pitcher and Unity started to pour
She looked at me with a crooked smile and said,
"Baby, how much freedom can you afford?"
I pulled some lent from my right pocket and nine pennies from the other
…
offered her what I had only to discover

...
that nine cents worth of Freedom
will not set you free
That which I have always imagined,
Will continue to elude me

Elephants & Ants

This morning
...
this morning, there was no hanging my
"over"
over a shower rod
Shit, I miss my days of
Kung Fu theater,
Kool Cups
&
Conjunction Junction
...
what's your function
...
following a fly Friday night
might
might have had breakfast with my blue
print prophecy of woman, while watching
Woody Wood Pecker and uh ...
Speed Racer, Chilly Willy and the Banana
Splits ...

shit, it's I miss my nights lusting a
black Pontiac dreaming of driving a
white drop top in Miami with a theme song
in
every life scene sung by popular artist to
compliment my "cool"

Although Bo & Luke were country cousins
on my
"white" side when action overwhelmed me,
dare I get as incredible and green as
Farrigno when I could no longer control
Angry

days designed by Dreams Incorporated
and
nights marinated in myths of herbs made
from Imagination
Meeting Mark & Mindy,
Mr. Kotter,
Mr. & Mrs. Ropper, Janet, Jack & Cindy …
the A Team, the Hearts,
Magnum P.I. and these two cats called
Hawk & Spenser at this little bar in

Boston where everyone knows your name
while
Moonlighting ...
it was crazy baby

games ... they weren't me then and they aren't me now
somehow, I've managed this life this long
it's been so long,
but you ... you remind me of who I am
you give me a reason to sing a new song
every time I die in your eyes, I ...
I recall who I am and what I've come from,
as I'm blinded by the Saturday Sun
hiding in a shear blue
...
on a smoky Friday night, Clarity capsized my sail ...
I sent an S.O.S. ... it sent me to Sanity's shore ...
said all of that to say
I Love You

I've always had extreme difficulties operating by Fool's definitions ...

trading transmissions of intentions to
produce fruitful futures for
past transgressions ... regressions, not
many,
but I'd be lying if I offered that I didn't
have any
I don't mind being fooled by a smile ...
getting over those is easy ...
it's simply that Experience has taught me
that
we just can't handle camouflaged
character flaws
meticulously maturated merely in order to
please me ...
that's all

See,
every time I die in your eyes,
I recall who I am and what I've come from
as I'm blinded by the Saturday Sun
hiding in a shear blue
on a smoky Friday night, Clarity capsized
my sail ...
I sent an S.O.S. and swam to Sanity's shore
Hell, said all of that to simply say that

I Love You

It is impossible for U 2 allow any1 else 2
satisfy U, unless u allow 'self' 2
satisfy self
Satisfaction only comes when
circumstances
chances U 2 embrace U
Embrace entails acceptance of the
marriage between
Honesty and Justice, whose offspring is
Fairness ... there, lest we forget,
is our purpose

Therefore, I cherish each breath I'm
blessed 2 breathe
See, with my ears
Hear, with my hands
Feel, with my eyes
Try, is a three lettered Failure's
synonym for success
press, towards the aft and
leave behind the stern
yearn, for more than merely to making it
to shore, but be seduced by life and the

peace "heaven on Earth" David
wrote about brings

As I stand staring at my own reflection,
projected images of dead skin find their
way to the floor, to create a bed of what
my soul has labeled "rejection"
and I recall who I am
And much like the myth that I am,
the past provides fuel to consume the
matter removed from me making my
voyage
visible to the ant who would
hold up an elephant
and
'WE'
rise
blinded by the Saturday Sun
in a shear blue
because last night, Clarity capsized my sail
…
I sent out an S.O.S. and swam to Sanity's
shore
no mass, no more must I continue to
drown in this

cesspool of stupidity
hell, I simply said all of that to stress that
eye love me

Excuse Me Miss

she hadn't noticed him,
but he knew her in a crowded room with
her back turned
the manner in which every strand nestled
gently at her whim on her head
the manner in which her infectious smile
diseased onlookers like
medusa...as opposed to stone,
gazing upon her was a one-way trip to
bliss
and
direct eye contact made magic genies wish
the manner in which fine linen was blessed
beyond bliss to
kiss her frame in such a way, angels en
route to carry out
the creator's grand plan strayed

he knew her

he knew her in a crowded room
in a dark valley, she would be the night's light
along the shore, she would serve as the tower that will save a sailor's life
in a desert, she would be the mirage that allowed a dying traveler might

he knew her
he knew
that for every mistake he made,
she forgave
rocket scientist, not required
she was the best compliment to every
well-wishing deed he has in operation
that complicated path that had been
muddied by mess from every angle,
she paved
and
when a spiritual refuge was required to provide
sanctuary from sordid soul snatchers that fronted for friends
she
and

she alone afforded him a place to stay

he knew her
he knew that rainy nights reminded him
how well his
hands caressed the contours of her
caramel skin
minus ever actually touching her at all
hence when there's a chill in the summer
breeze,
the hair on his hands stand tall
he knew that the Texas heat hinted
towards
the exigent temperature of the furnace
they call foreplay creates
and although he would never be
acknowledged by NASA,
he could describe in great detail what it is
like to travel to
Orion and approximately how long it is
going to take
he knew how sick and tired he got sick
and tired of sleeping alone
how does one attain peace, when a portion
of who

you have grown to become is gone?
bears all things
believes all things
hopes all things
relationships don't fail because we
"simply don't try"
they fail because the possibilities fell
through the bottom of dreams
she restores my soul
provides a personal paradise
Heaven, through you
to make my incomplete complicated
simplicity whole
i've done, you know that, i do
before 'we' even began, we were one
i saw the beauty in a satisfied fantasy
did you not see it to?
let's live the dream baby,
find pleasure in the possibilities,
make time non-existent lady
and
live "in" love till Love says enough daisy

seems a fitting find, that he should be
blessed by such a beautiful sealer

an aesthetically perfectly pleasing
schematic healer
he knew
that he had unearthed a rare heirloom
from a lost Atlantis treasure
beyond measure, many had vaguely
attempted
but fewer had dared tried
but all before receiving one of God's
greatest blessings,
had been denied
he knew
she was the camouflaged craftsman who's
hands re-shaped the
master key

smiling from the nirvana,
he gently wrapped his hungry hands
around the
hips he had lusted dust till dawn
excuse me miss
but you
you remind me

free falling

lately,
I find myself inundated with images
reminding me of tomorrow's uncertainty
that
feels for familiarity from yesterday
I was...am...and will always be a bridge
troubled or not
waters lie below
and lo
my reflection is that of a man
I scarcely know
unrecognizable to thee
is he who resembles me
and I
I find myself sitting with my back to the door,
because I simply cannot face it

I find myself lining my sights to moving
targets
that ride with the wind
I pray my aim holds true
hell,
when the lights get low
how well does your halo glow?
maintenance matters you know
like watching dripping code confused by
salty breezes blown in by
righteously wicked winds
praying for the day engulfed shores are
greeted by grateful waves
that wash away eroded emotions stained
from sun-dried sin
yes
something serious this way comes
waiting in windows
staring at shadows
looking for lost love
we are but dust living in the roux of pale
stale light
I find myself flirting with frustration,
afraid fool's gold is all there is left
right wing conspiracy

being the bastard child of Anarchy,
I am compelled to believe
you do not want to be a pawn in a king's game
you are nothing more than an unfortunate
casualty with limited liability
the failure of expectancy invites
mismanagement of the golden rule
what is the burden that contains the beast?
how well do you feel the world
wrapped in the wrong hue?
life certainly cannot be about reviewing
your mistakes,
merely to rest in rapprochement
tainted by experience, yet justified by faith
does not a misdirected truth not sound
like a lie?
just listen
just listen to the characters in your eye
a man's life should never be measured in
terms of right and wrong
for in life, there are no simple answers
however, the degree to which he sways
from
one side to the other should be sufficient

just as ones worth is never limited to a single act,
the same should be considered when rendering his purpose
if what we do in life is truly echoed in eternity,
then it is ones aggregated story that would be contemplated
when a man sees his end, he needs to know the purpose of his living
so that his soul ascends in peace
ultimately, we are all clay
from the Earth, we begin
and it is the Earth that shall embrace our end
it is said dirt washes easier than blood
how hard will you rub during your dissolving days?
lately,
I find myself inundated with images reminding me of
tomorrow's uncertainty that feels for familiarity in now

Hatin' Remedy

While you're screaming
"Brother, Brother"
You're running your black ass under
Some dark covers
Claiming to be something you're not,
but you want me to jump in your hot pot
Oh yeah, you down for the cause...
Hold up, stop the press, wait, let me put a
pin in right here
and pause
See, you got the color, the gear, and all
that stuff
and you're wearing your bald head, bald
fade,
or braids and kickin' up dust!
But the fallacy of your dry ass reality...
is it real, or is it Memorex?
And you call yourself on the matter an

authority!
Just because what you heard, said, or read
doesn't equal what I believe...
why you wanna knock me
because of what you conceive?
Ignorance beget ignorance,
Brother,
don't you know,
and you have the audacity to stand before
me and put me on the cutting floor?
Simple minds make simple thoughts
and simple folks open simple vaults
So, while you're trying to break my back
and
turn me around,
I want to feed this to you and hope you
can keep this down
Dispute me if you will and try me if you
must,
but what you read it seems you TRUST
You say my author has lied and distorted,
but how do you know your author has not
disordered?
I sincerely hope I caused turbulence in
your ocean,

while I pull the pin out and set this
message
in motion
Brother, can you relate?
Let's find common ground for progress
sake,
instead of reasons to
try to hate!!!

I Hope So

I cannot endure to watch you depart
However, I embrace each moment you enter
To be honest, I simply enjoy watching you move...
hoping you are never moving too far from me, but
allowing me the opportunity to see you return to me
is truly a treasure
While we are dissociated, is our association
a part of your mental process?
Have I occupied your mind at sometime during the day
that makes you say cum here?
I hope so

Is the rapture of impeding plights of erect
illusions
caught in your sight?
I hope so
Do you long for the day we lay on
the shores of Pleasure Island to
hear love say welcome?
I hope so
So much so, that solidarity is ashamed
of its incompleteness standing in the
shadows our unity
While you are away from me,
I have imagined us and our possibilities
I have heeded the call of probability
I have smelled the scent of attraction
I have savored the flavor of desire
I have sensed the embrace of passion
I have seen the candle lit lust
I have envisioned that which
can be & hopefully is us
In my mind, we have traveled to a
joyous impasse making gratification
last beyond bodily existence
Traveling to our souls' sensation
Breakfast in Sedona

Lunch in Savannah
Dinner & Desert in Salzburg
With pertinent pleasantries hosting this
magnanimous reception
where we like rain to earth
complement each other
I have imagined us
Residing in the state of grace
where pain is replaced by peace
I have imagined us
Seizing the fortress of fortitude
to keep our hearts at ease
I have imagined us
Caressing the careless whisper of the wind
that blows in to bless each new day we
partake of this notion of US
All alone, I imagine us
I hope you have done the same
So much so, that you are never
ashamed to cry out my name
Or to testify to the fact that I am the one
who places that smile on your face
Natural and unforced baby,
Let us be
I imagine you

You imagine me?
I hope so

In Passing

I was born under a shy sun
a mad moon
a contrary constellation
I was born amidst an angry wind
during a dark December
I am a child of the night
I am the son of Bastet
cousin to Osiris and Thanos
cousin to Isis and Venus
grandchild of Ra
I have been blind from birth,
yet blessed to see what many cannot
I have lived in the abyss of love,
and it smelled like Hell
I have drowned in the possibilities,
being reborn in the reality that nothing is
infinite
nor is anything permanent

time is a luxury,
just as space is a comfort
neither are afforded to any man,
so why should concerns precede the inevitable
I have been vulnerable to inadequacies and ignorance...
trapped in a labyrinth of lies
led through confusion by Desire
with a noose around my neck,
I have been drug into a den of
solemn souls and menial minds that use
space synonymous with time only to understand
that comprehension is a blessing
that many have not received
although perceived notions are good for stroking egos,
those that dwell in this den will never
align with a ray of light
lost is a sense of security and refuge is not conferred
faith is deferred and affliction is perennial
prayer is not an option, but a demand
at hand are my kin who listen and then

offer dungeon lullaby's to Allah
like a whisper in the wind

I am just passing through
I am just passing through this
nebulous that keeps optimism and hope
at the depths of enchained emotions
at the bottom of enslaved imaginations
I am just passing through
I become the Patron Saint of
Procrastination
and
Exacerbation
the stench of stupidity fills the
air, and there...rather here
is where knowledge is
suffocated
and
delirium
sets in
I am compelled to consume the few
graces that remain
In this present station of consternation,
I am a hostage in a depression of
confrontation...

prisoner of the people of questions
what lies beneath my skin
is the composition of a god
fused with the ability of an infant
I am the sum total of stupidity,
with a twist of integrity

but, I am just passing through
In passing,
I am hearing what must be done,
and those things that I need to do
among the tears of sorrow
and the dungeon lullaby's,
I am hearing the cry's of sedated souls
moans of grief echo in the hollow halls of
my mind
I struggle to stay sane on this plane of
mediocrity
what is lost here, cannot be reclaimed
like a virgins first night
or
a warriors first kill
thrill of the sweet innocence that
once existed prior to this overflow
of ignorance, is now a memory...still

I find it hard to stay fair
something lingers in the stillborn air,
and it smells like
Death

she stands at the door
and will not allow me to pass
Hell,
I thought I was
just passing through

Caujikwurx

I'm telling you...
(she was telling me, really?)

if you believe in the impossible,
how do you allow the tangible
to inhibit the probable?
like reminding me to be religious,
although this war is spiritual
if you're calling a spade a spade,
how am I wrong for making mention of the
malarkey
Maliciousness made?
soul's been singed, mind remolded and
sanity scolded
perhaps, more offended than anything
nothing never means everything,
till it means sumthing

so, how does one profanely protest an assumption
systematically set in ghost mode to snickerly satisfy
sumone else's selfish insinuations?
everyone has a story…a soundtrack…a symphony
to say what sumone's isn't,
is to assert what yours is
what you give is what you get
how else am eye to respond to blatant disregard and profound disrespect?
my matching the mode met,
is no more wrong than being right in calling a vanity mirror a lie
and why?
like a lost lover looking for an everlasting love,
loose lips precedes an untamed tongue
eyem addicted to understanding
craving wisdom in every ignorant act
found that
facts are figures for statistics
and
reality

like beauty
is employed by the beholder
when working with a bolder brilliance,
minimize the amount of contrast
enhance the hue
and let the levels do what they do
greatly improving the images intelligence
eye can only imagine the objective
usefulness
of tyrannical treachery
the madness stupidity offers, is but a
token of immeasurable despair
when demeaning symbols are easily slung
to create the greatest amount of
destruction,
what compliments care?
Disparity never allows Delirium to travel
alone for too long
so always be prepared for a
foul stench in the air
the strain of misguided persecutions
remove restraints, allowing for the easy
extraction of useless sacraments
tell me...
how does one find comfort in confusion?

in a world of popular public opinion polls
prostituted politicians and false positive
preachers
what is pleased?
the price of infamy is pain
when heaven is pimped as a consolation
prize
long as eye serve as a hypocrite's assistant
tell me...
how shall eye proceed?
dense hearts numb perspective cognition,
like translucent logic irradiates retention
remorse is all that resides
pride
set aside
eye am rightly left alone
holding my hot cup of
empty apathetic empathy
perhaps eye am a hypocrite's prodigal son
eye am the patron
saint of uncanny shit
whoa is me

Satin Stains

Flashes of familiar places
imprison my thoughts in
unlit lighthouses my mind
abandoned years ago
I am forced to recall a
distant design
held hostage in collapsed caverns
concerning myself with the
glyphs I seemingly missed
on now severely damaged walls
Overloaded by illusions,
I suffer a massive depression
desperately pleading
to comprehend it all
seeking satisfaction in unseen
arenas where antagonist are
not needed

I am a lone ranger
robbed of my costume, weapon and trusty
steed
an ambiguous advocate
is all that I am
destined to be
whoa is me
that I should fall victim
to a jealous zealot's envy
publically mocked and humiliated
to the degree even those who
would call themselves family
eventually shun me
can this not be prophesy?
what carpenter is not an artist or
artist not a carpenter in his own right?
devoid of light,
reality is warped by
every ignorant character covered
I consider alternatives
that read like alternate realities
second generation surrogates
like dimensions birthed
in a universe of twisted truths
if a line's design detours at will,

can we ever see it straight?
forged from forgiveness,
these truths fade with
every grain of salt that falls
within the glass
choosing to embroider the
more pleasant moments,
vibrant painting's borders do fade
If never restored
the past is only as beautiful
as experience exposes it to me
hindsight allows for enhanced clarity,
but during the act...I can only accept
the tales told as truths offensively sold me
Irony
continuously calling this hell
well, maybe the "Heaven on Earth" David
spoke of
is Atlantis, but does it really matter?
fact the probability exists, pre-treats for a
proper quest
at best,
what could I lose?
yet, claiming it nonexistent,
is living the love of a lie

filtered facts are imitations
a perplexed Memorex of extracted acts
twisted tongues often
mutilate astute transmissions,
pre-treating sound logic
with torpid revisions
how brilliant are cloaked colors
captured in callous light?
how black & white was the world when
God whispered let there be sight?
when every action is captioned by foul
foot-notes,
what are accurate quotes?
when parts are improperly identified,
how is it possible to produce
an accurate sum?
Love let's Grace soothe the pain
living brings and
soulfully
wholefully
pray
'thy will be done'

Sounds of Blackness

She spoke in soft accents
that mirrored laments
Phonemes, it seems, which
infiltrate my dreams
that fail to leave me alone
affording my feeble mind time to
construct a fabled place to call home
And although her tongue is better,
her eyes give it a try
her tone, willingly offers her tell
her moans, intercept each lie
Beseeched by orbs that submerges me like
sand,
I ignore the cautious call
Her soul's windows, worn like stained
glass,
are levied by lids that lapse with longing
like bass notes,
she needs the bottom to fall

the light banter
the conscious quest
craving every delightful detail
her lips eagerly wet
she strives to consume it all
I fit her favorite flavor
featuring a fragrance her senses
cannot sway
fondle me along your roof
and find I'm never too far away
Drowning deep in Desire's well,
she is forced to savor
every tantalizing taste
needing my tip to touch her like Braille
she embroiders her ecstasy in all caps
as to not allow a second of pleasure
to go to waste

Yes, indeed
the lady has needs
and she pleads for me
to be more than merely in her

I be the blood her heart
profusely pumps with wanted pain

increasing the intensity of every
erotic organ she owns
as I occupy each artery
and ventilate every vein
I be Captain of a pirated ship
probing her paradise for a misplaced pearl
finding an interior lining
open for mining
in a lost lagoon hidden to this world
dive into her free flowing fluids of amenity
that have been masterfully drafted
satiated by an oasis of love
lustfully crafted
wanting me to dig deep past her
chocolate covered caverns
and dwell within the realm of her
caramel coated home
She wants me to record mystory
in high definition with vibrant
hues impressed sagaciously inside her
Her hand extended to mine
amidst the roof of her
sacred dome
I be her beat
I be her core

I be the manifest destiny
her hands grip for more
I be the cooling flame
she emits with each breath to gain
sanctuary for her soul
I design and we erect a monument
on Mount Us where a plethora
of realities unfold
She wants me sitting sideways
on the apex of her axis
dancing uncontrollably
serenaded by the
sensuous sounds of our blackness

Yes, indeed
the lady has needs
and she pleads for me
to be more than merely in her

Sticks & Stones

she said my words,
were words
nothing more than mere characters to
convey a communication
words
letters strung together to better
express thoughts i should digress
words
hollow characters that lurk in the corners
of the
night like ghost
tauntingly haunting you to recall choices
made prior to,
in hopes that the future won't meet you
doing the most
words
believing sticks and stones may break her
bones,

words were vicarious vices used as
weapons of mass destruction
minus the boom
leaving her warheads both empty &
weightless,
they were always allotted a little wiggle
room
frequently referring to the need for
something she can feel,
words have become symbolic systems
that serve as personal propaganda
and since she is not running for office
now requires something way more real
now needing much more than my
words
however, something I heard had me stuck
on stupid
and slapped me as strange
no, I don't know you, do i?
never met you, did i?
introduced to you
however, when we converged i never
merged with you
someone
something close to you

just not you, true?
you offer information as if sending
a telegraphed transmission by
way of horseback
but still you wish for me
to run to you
pray tell
who am i running to?
when you hide in undiscovered territories
never introduced,
what is there to be explored?
how fit for hueman habitation is the
uncharted environment?
is the zone bright only at
night in the blood moon's twilight?
when walls are adorned with ethereal ink,
what does one perceive?
how does one comprehend that which
cannot be seen?
if the best view of you for me to see is
sought in social circles,
then perhaps that is the wall i have need to
read
how important to you must I be, when I
have never been

worthy of you?
i cannot be your perfect peace
i am your putrid pain
undesired and expertly extracted
a past participle that allegedly
contained no gain
surgically removed from you, defining me
a disease
you cannot even lay with me like
"we" set your soul at ease,
hence the need to be free
hell, even needing a frenzy to fall asleep,
i found myself forever wondering would i
ever become for you,
what you are to me?
a blessed blanket of security
apparently,
your world does not require me
request,
maybe
but need…hella hard to believe
i am the shiny juju you sit on your
shoulder for others to see
and when the weight is no longer
welcome,

returned to your dresser to simply be
i cannot be the air you breath
i am the climax in your unwritten
symphony
you were the only defined ray of sunshine
in my darkened world
and now, I'm left to lay
in the luxury of letters
that fade before my eyes
your words

Do not mourn for me,
simply let me be

It is moments like these,
that defines this mortality
It is not for the one who
leaves for whom we should grieve,
but for the one who
enters who has been deceived
When a child leaves home,
does not your soul moan?
When that child returns,
does not your joy burn?
So let it be with me,
when on that day you see
me travel back home
Ashes to Ashes & Dust to Dust

Since there is a prepared place for me,
I trust you will find comfort
in knowing that my time is up
Learning has ceased
The journey is at its end
The time for rejoicing is now
Now... ascension begins
Leaving this tainted existence
for a greater plain, though
the spirit transforms, the
memories remain the same
The suffering that once was,
no longer is...
Therefore, let not your heart be troubled
nor let your mind be weary
When you were without my presence,
I was still near thee

So, do not mourn for me,
simply let me be
still

Metamorphosis

On the banks of Ubiquity,
   a soft sun sets
 and I am resting on the heels
    of my burdens
   Entranced by the ebb & flow from the
Sea of Fools
Kemetic notions of pleasures not
embraced
  affords me the misery of
 acknowledging my menial existence
    and I question my
   submission among these saturated
cesspools
Schooled in the ways of Adam,
   I too have falsely accused others
 for mistakes I have made
    which directs me towards

a destructive design of denial that detours truth
How can sanity be sought, searching for shadows in the dark?
This insistent inquisition mirrors a prominent Spanish expedition ...
I pray my fortune is fairly favorable
Measured by the maniacal manner of man I am,
success seems to seek
a less than forgiving path to attain refuge and
I am left limp after a trial of errors not noted
In the script of my life
What am I to become?

The Lost City

A certain child collected
his goods
and went to a far off country
He learned the principles of
clarity, but failed to
acquire its application
Give me what is mine now
I can wait no longer,
was his cry
With knowing being half the
battle, he was forced to
endure the trials that
ignorance brings
A content song did he sing:
"if it is to be, it shall be"
But it was not good enough
for the lad
This song only made him mad

He thought,
"I have a lot to offer,
but I have no takers"
Is my journey all for not?
Is my happiness a fleeting moment?
Can clarity be so laborious?
By performing all the right duties
(in his mind)
his actions were all wrong
(in reality)
Yes, I was that prodigal child
and the country was called Love
Since I've met you though,
application has not been
an issue
To squander your love,
is a sin for which there
is no atonement
To replace your love,
is like searching for
the lost city of Atlantis
I may have a physical description,
but I will never come close
I will only find ruins and
a few remains

clues
Only clues, but never
solving the mystery
To hold onto your love
is what I seek to do
For I know there is nothing more
treasured in this world, than
the gift you have given me
For to love and be loved,
is a quest we all entertain
But I may end my journey now,
because I have found what
I have searched
long and hard for
you
my lost city

Colors

My heart's flag is set at half-mast
and
somewhere between the crevices
...
my mind tells me
"this too, shall pass"
However, that thought
may soon be replaced
with a White Flag

Surrender
(seemingly)
is a compelling option to conflicting
crusades
campaigns that no longer have value
should never be prolonged
Accepting the obvious, is like standing in
the eye of the storm

No matter what direction you move,
torrential pain is soon to set
So, how can I be content with
my utter displacement

For
my back ... is an open forum
for those who would lie
my front ... is being strong enough
to never just die
But I ...
I cannot accept defeat
knowing full well that
I have been beat

I am battered
I am bruised
I am a misused
toy for those who would offer pleasure
yet yield sorrow
tell me that a better day,
I shall soon see
then, offer tomorrow is a day not promised
to them **OR** me

...

and I wade

I wade in the water
awaiting a sign
I wade in the water
awaiting all that **IS** mine
I wade in the water
drowning from my struggle to sustain
and no matter how hard I fight,
I cannot escape the failure to maintain
I wade
wondering just how long I must wait
for my lifeline
and
every second that ticks away
I know
I am losing time

Hence
my heart's flag is set at half-mast
and
somewhere between the crevices
my mind tells me
"this too, shall pass"
And as the sun sets, guards prepare

my mast
for surrender
and
I die knowing that **THIS** affliction
will no longer last

Altered Reality

Just 8 months ago,
he was basking in the glow of being the
fourth member of his family to complete
his basic educations
Constellations danced for his endeavors,
however that elation would not last long
Those that make decisions, decided that
he would be better off serving a society
that still looked at him as less than
but never equal to
A few times during his short days, he was
amazed by being regarded as a man
But be damned if every time he thought
his condition had improved, a closer
examination communicated that he had
only been fooled
A fraction of a man with a magazine in one
and an M-16 in the other

his hand held like toys
Constantly being reminded of his position in this chain by everyone around him when they referred to him by boy
And although he had graduated high school with a 4.0 average, his suggestions were never good enough to try
But being that he was a boy, he became an expendable scout who was good enough finally ...
good enough to die
To quiet the suicidal soul within, he sought altered realities smoking & shooting everything he could get his hands on because the future his past promised him could, would never be
So, he sought modified materialism altered realities

Just 8 months ago,
the only things that infiltrated his system were
soul-food, Kool-Aid, and polluted oxygen now days, MRE rations, whiskey, and Mary Jane are dominant

Fighting to forget the shit he had done the day before was becoming a losing battle and creating too much pain
The weed was not working anymore ... that is when he decided he would take a ride on a unicorn: cocaine
For a really tight trip to get him lit, he would down a little southern whiskey, smoke a pound of weed, shoot some horse and drop some acid
See, the whiskey relaxed his trembling tensions ...
The weed removed his nervous apprehensions ...
The coke ransomed the concealed inhibitions ...
But the acid was needed to silence the hidden hunters bullets when they wisped by his ears to detour intruder retention
Everything he ingested was not for extravagance ... it was essential
Prudential faith he had been fed, afforded him no grace because killing is a sin & he was stuck in a
lose : lose

position
There was no way this lost soul would win
The sweet innocence that his past
provided, could no longer be regained
the dwindling future of being an avid
addict seemed more likely to attain
Having lost everything, he could find
nothing in his fruitless future to gain
So, after meeting with an orange agent
and being rescued from a fire fight where
he had witnessed four bullets penetrate a
tree, but not before they had punctured
his Lt.'s skull & extracted his brains, he
hesitantly boarded the helo ... the sweet
chariot that swung low to take him to
camp, only to return the next day with a
new Lt. and possibly go thru the same
thing
As they reached their peak to avert the
gooks gunfire, he knew he would never get
any higher
Taking the last bit of acid he had left, he
wanted to make things right
Picking his head up from his hands, he
stood erect ... walked over to the opened

hatch, grabbed the hand rail and I suspect
...
He wanted to try to fly the rest of the way
to Heaven, maybe God would give him a
pass
But he had not received a set of wings yet
... I wonder ... how long would that
euphoric feeling truly last?

Hell?!?
He had been there and back on
two tours of duty, and the poor soul was
only 19
I hope he found permanence in his
altered reality
and
flown far beyond his
fading dreams

Pink Slip

I've got my pen in my right hand
and my pad in the left
"Your services are no longer needed"
is the heading, and at the bottom ...
"much success"
I regret to inform you is followed by a
blank line,
name insertion,
it's about that time
You have been given this notice,
because the hour has come to past for you
to dip ...
beat it, bounce, move on ...
you've received a pink slip

The first time I had to pull out my pad, it
cut me to the core
A friend, well an associate ...

someone who decided they didn't want to
be so accommodating anymore
He did some shit I wouldn't expect from
an enemy
Pulled some 'greater' than player hatin'
bull,
and thought that I wouldn't see
Instead of being a man, he acted like a
little ole "b"
Did his deed, smiled in my face and
"What up man"
was all he had to say to me!
This fool pulled a bitch move, and I'm
supposed to act like we're still cool?
Ice-T told me a long time ago though that
"some of the niggas are bitches too"
I tried to rationalize the shit, but I could
find no valid excuse
It was nothing more than a bitch move that
a bitch used ...
and for that, I gotta slip you!

With my pen in my right hand
and my pad in the left
"Your services are no longer needed"

is the heading, and at the bottom ...
"much success"
I regret to inform you is followed by a blank line,
name insertion,
it's about that time
You have been given this notice,
because the hour has come for you to dip
...
beat it, bounce, move on dawg!!!
You've received a pink slip

I aint ever been one to freak behind a love gone bad,
especially when it was behind some good that a brother never had
It's not the love lost that gets to me,
that's actually to be expected
But the problem lies with the way we got to that point,
the shit we did to neglect it!
Ok ... so, say I got beyond her past
After being raped by her cousin at 12, she simply gave up the ass
By the time she got to me,

I think my number was like 60
I paid it all no never mind, because
the girl had still been traumatized all this
time
In my eyes, she simply needed help and
love made me stay
I'd always remind her, her past would
never make me walk away
But the problem kicked in when the true
lies got serious
From time to time, even her own family
knew this girl was delirious!
The one that said I raped her was no fun ...
and the one that had me beat her in the
head with a gun left me stunned!
One morning, she told me that she loved
me right after she blew my brains ... and
that very damn evening was when the
restraining order came and confirmed my
worst fear ...
this chick is insane!
It was nothing more than a bitch move that
a bitch used ...
and for that, I gotta slip you

With my pen in my right hand
and my pad in the left
"Your services are no longer needed"
is the heading, and at the bottom ...
"much success"
I regret to inform you is followed by a
blank line,
name insertion,
It's about that time
You have been given this notice,
because the hour has passed for you to
dip
beat it, bounce, move on trick!!!
You've received a pink slip

Even family can wreck your shit ...
a drunk father or a crack head cousin can
certainly make life a trip!
I think back to my CD collection valued at
five grand easy
There's nothing like a sax solo, bass line
or smooth piano to please me
From Motley Crue to Mozart, my music
was tight!

I had a song for every occasion, and if it
wasn't on the rack ...
it'd be there by the end of the night
One night, 3 boxes of fifty CD's sprouted
wings and took flight ...
and since I knew CD's don't fly unless you
throw them,
sumthin' wasn't right!
this funky bastard tried to deny the
obvious and play me for a damn fool
Guess he was too fucked up to remember
that
I teach teachers how to teach school
I was just about to let the shit go & say
that is that ...
went to a store to purchase some used
CD's,
and there my shit was on the rack!
I asked the manager who sold the CD's,
and we looked at the damn list
Wouldn't you know
my crack head cousin!
now, I'm really pissed
It was nothing more than a bitch move that
a bitch used

and for that, I gotta slip you!

With my pen in my right hand
and my pad in the left
"Your services are no longer needed"
is the heading, and at the bottom ...
"much success"
I regret to inform you is followed by a
blank line,
name insertion,
it's about that time
You have been given this notice,
because the hour has come to pass for you
to dip ...
beat it, bounce, move on cuz!!!
You've received a pink slip
See, it really doesn't matter who it is
NO ONES EXEMPT
From fake ass friends to lucid lovers, to
fraudulent family ...
anyone can get slipped
So, the next time you notice a bitch move
that a bitch used, and they're fucking up
your world view ...
get your pen in your right hand

and your pad in your left
and tell them calmly
I GOTTA SLIP YOU!!!

Cybernetic Cypher

Back in the days,
social media used to sound like
dedications read over radio waves
featuring the occasional shout-out
in B-lunch during happy school days
fast forward...the future
even a fool can find five seconds of fame
sucked inside Pandora's toy box
playing into online games

subjectivity is the enemy
when one honors not the past
an arrogant ass is subjected to planting
his shoes in sugar fields
fighting for a future
where solidity disfigures the real
falsely claiming to be the producer
of something someone can feel
find a paved path within the grass
and like false prophets before him,

offer the plantation's master a new deal
where is the symmetry?
wherein lies the beauty that
professes to be poetry?
when it is palpable,
it is plain to see

my prose poses poetically
pleases the palette when it leaves my
tongue
like I French kissed artistically
when I dream, my guardian should
translate
said scenes in a sacred book of antiquities
when hunting dragons,
it is best to tread bravely
seeking,
is not the same
when it comes to a name
all out of biscuits
if you are gravy, I am game
horizontal line on a vertical plain,
who are you really and what are you
saying?

like Africa calling America her mother
wearing Jerusalem as a choker
and the Vatican as a chain
Eden dissolved to blood diamonds
that dwell in her rock salt soul
bold are the elevations that freely
flow from the pretender's tongues
bringing only a beaten brown baton
to a fight restricted to heavy machine guns
be super sensitive when claiming to be
Neo
in the flesh
are you truly the one?
when your catalogue contains
more than misinformed claps & off-beat
snaps
perhaps
till then, you are nothing more than
a sewer rat tracing for turtles
victim of a shreddar's trap
ego so inflated, your forehead tells tall
tales
your ass honestly cannot cash
tongue can't color in translucent lines
that hides behind imaginary checks

in an undercover boss' stash
contrary to popular pixilated belief,
there is no such truth as taming a dragon
that is an embellished urban myth
like praying for the loyalty of a pit
heard a good bitch always requires a
love lick
are you absolutely
positively
one hundred percent assuredly
needing now to be when you get hit?

Love Dance

I want to dance with a lovebird in
paradise
Fly by petrified trees with black leaves,
so that our dance can restore lost things
like
lost thoughts
lost dreams
lost life
Fly by run-dry waterfalls and wells,
so that our dance cast eternal spells
like
peace
love
happiness
Fly by dead foliage and barren lands,
so that our dance can be consuming
like
sifting sands

encompassing all and denying none
Combining time, space and grace in one
My bird of prey and I dance
till our joy is more than consensual
we dance
till moments spent in bliss are 180 times
past sensual
we dance
till the never ending might of the sun is
blinded by our light
we dance
My bird of prey and I dance
She extends herself to me, and I
accept her completely
her soft wings
her full breast
her thick thighs
her jaded eyes
She absolves my soul absolutely, taking
me places Morpheus can only imagine
making me crave her like crème de cacao
covered strawberry delights
Appealing to my eyes
stationary or in flight
This crowned jewel of Africa arouses every

sensation of mine, and I would
have to be blind not to notice
that her amendments to love are
deliberate
She wants me
I want her
So, if that I would travel a thousand
thermals to simply
see her
be near her
be afforded the chance to dance with her
then that's what I shall do
I want to dance with a lovebird in
paradise
if but for only a moment of the day
if but only for one night

Sentimental

I am not concerned about the
things we have been through...
they have already been discussed
You should know by now that
you have all of my love
I am not concentrating on the
things we are lacking...
they will come in time
You should know by now that
whatever I have... is yours
I am not contemplating the
things we have discovered...
they have always been there
You should know by now that
this union is undeniable
There are some things
I am inclined to question
There are a few things

I am learning to cope with
But,
there are a couple of things
I know

I know that I love you
and
I know that you love me
This fact is reinforced every time
I look in your eyes
I hear your voice
I feel your touch
This joy is not in question
Just keep me in your dreams
somewhere in your thoughts
One day,
we shall live in love
This is the hope that I rise to
every morning
Let no one take this joy
from me
This is all I have

Love
always & forever

The Successful Failure

A collective hallucination of
ignorance stupefies me like
a clean and sober Hendrix
asking if I'm experienced
leaving me in pieces
soul bankrupt
mind corrupt
Broken into pieces, like
stale cracker crumbs on a cold
kitchen floor, I'm reliving a
fairy tale
I just wish someone would have told me
the truth in my youth... that
Humpty Dumpty choked on his own
yoke, that's why he had great fall
from a wall he was trespassing on...
and
the tried and true Emergency Medical

Response Team was too damn slow
on the scene, so as a result, he
passed cuz his ignant ass tied a
loose noose around his throat
It made perfect sense at the time,
however, his benign ignorance
slipped somewhere between stupidity
and intelligence and he himself slipped
into darkness… not because of the
act he committed, but because he
figured his yoke was finished
And I'm not certain which curtain
should be unfurled first
Despair or Desire
And I'm not sure what's worst
the fact that I've thought the same
thoughts
or
the knowledge of knowing I've committed
the same act

Even when I seemingly succeed, I've
failed in some way
And on any given day, I can view
my pluralized faux pas

Oh lawd what did I do?
what did I do?
what did I do to deserve this?
I know my life is fucked & I aint
shit, but please hear a failure's plea
I've become nothing more than an
oxymoron... the result of one of the
Creator's sad jokes
I hear
"suicide is painless
it brings on many changes
and I can take or leave it if I please"
on my knees, I yield... I yield not to my
insecurities, but to the pain the blues
brings when there's more than a touch
of reality in the song the singer sings
Like Sam Cooke repeating a change is
gone come
or
Riley King reminding me that the thrill is
gone
or
Donny Hathaway reiterating that someday
we'll be free

In reality, the failure finds a connection in all three
because my thrill been gone…
left home on broken wings and my change will come when I'm free
free from this pathetic existence of being a successful failure
No, life for me aint been no crystal stare
so, let me take this glass eye and do the best I can with what I've got

Acknowledgements

Life is a masterful mystery filled with a plethora of uncertainties. For me to say that one event supersedes another is to offer a great untruth. I will say that all paths have led to this point, where I am more than comfortable with who the Grand Architect has made me to be. His plans have trumped my childhood ideas as to who I would become. For instance, my time among the poetic community was supposed to be limited to a couple of years. I was to write one or two collections, then begin my novel phase. After over fifteen years of performance poetry, I think it is sufficient to say that those were 'novel' ideas...pun intended.

I can confidently offer that my journey has been an enlightening one filled with adventures I could have never dreamed. It was never my intention to be an integral part of this system for so long, but I am by no means disturbed by it either. There's nothing like the feeling of hearing someone offer that the words I've presented has helped them in their life's journey. I have often equated the process to a spiritual impasse, and the artists who adorn the stage are ministers of sorts. We are word playing painters who brush color in the lives of others. We are more than authors, we are edutainers...entertainers who educate along the way. We are alchemists and words are our weapons of choice.

This being the premise, my position in the system has been more than solidified. I am an artist and I am finally comfortable with the full knowledge of my impact on others. I am a wordsmith and my life is not limited to the page nor the stage...it is on display for the world to examine at will. That being the case, each and every person who has touched me, has had an impact on my world. Positively or negatively, each person who has been a part of my life shares the stage and the page with me. I salute you for being you and I thank you for letting me be me. These are but a few brief confessions of a simple soul and I am blessed to have you a part of my journey.